THE INTERNET
...Is and How to Use It

Enslow Publishing
101 W. 23rd Street
Suite 240
New York, NY 10011
USA

enslow.com

Tricia Yearling

WORDS TO KNOW

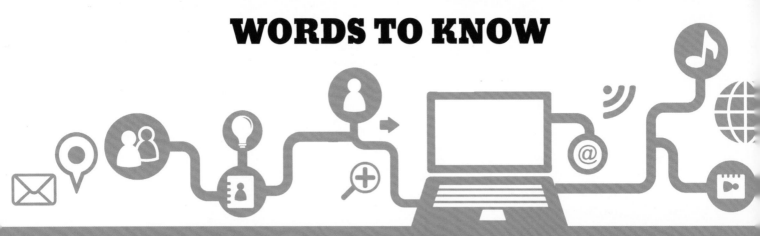

binary—A number system that uses only two numbers: 0 and 1. One binary number is called a bit.

data—Facts and other information.

domain name—The part of a network address that tells what group of computers it belongs to.

fiber optic lines—Special cables through which a large amount of information can travel.

network—A group of computers that are connected to each other.

packets—Units of data that are sent from one place on the Internet to another.

protocols— The rules by which data is put into order.

satellites—Special pieces of equipment that are sent into space to travel around Earth and send and receive information.

servers—Computer hardware that stores and presents web pages.

software—Instructions that tell a computer what to do.

CONTENTS

The Internet can
connect you to all
kinds of information
all over the globe!

What Is the Internet?

Do you watch shows on demand on a TV, a computer, or a tablet? Do you play video games online with friends? Do you talk or video chat with your grandma on Skype or gchat? If you answered yes, you use the Internet! The Internet is a huge network. A network lets computers send and receive data from other computers. The Internet connects computers all around the world.

A Network of Networks

The Internet is made up of many smaller networks. These networks are linked by satellites, fiber optic lines, and other kinds of cables. They are sometimes called the backbone of the Internet because they are the Internet's main support. Internet service providers, or ISPs, own these. People pay ISPs to be able to connect to the Internet.

Computers Talking to Each Other

Computers use special rules called protocols (pronounced PRO-tuh-calls) to talk to each other. There are two main protocols. The first is called TCP (transmission control

The Internet is sometimes called the net.

IP Address

All computers that are online have an IP address. The numbers of the IP address tell other computers what network that computer belongs to.

protocol). TCP puts data into groups called packets. TCP also makes sure the packets are put together in the right order. The second is called IP (Internet protocol). The IP labels each piece of data with a number. This works like a mailing address. The number tells the IP where the data needs to go. Then the IP moves it there.

Modems

Modems change your computer's language into sounds that can travel over the network. The sounds change back to language when they reach another modem.

Computer Language

A computer needs a modem to connect to the Internet. A modem is a tool that changes computer language into sounds. Those sounds travel over the network to another modem. That modem changes the sounds back into computer language. Some modems send and receive data slowly. Others, such as DSL modems and cable modems, send and receive data quickly. ISPs give modems to their customers.

What's on the Internet?

The Internet can allow you to do many different things. You can get help with your homework, watch movies, or play games. You can also listen to music and talk to people who live far away. To do these things, you use the World Wide Web.

The Net and the Web

Some people think the Internet and the World Wide Web are the same thing. But they're not! The Internet is a network that connects computers. The World Wide Web, or Web, is

Hyperlinks are words, phrases, or pictures that you click on to move to new web pages.

a collection of pages of information and files. These web pages are linked together. You can find them using the Internet.

Web pages are stored on servers. The web servers that store web pages each have their own IP address. This tells computers where the server is. It also tells computers what network the server belongs to. The numbers in the IP address are given a domain name. This makes it easier for people to remember the server's IP address.

All those web pages you visit are stored on servers. Severs are super fast computers. Sometimes entire rooms or buildings are used to store servers.

Using the Internet

A group of web pages are called a website. Every website has an Internet address. Internet addresses are called URLs (uniform resource locaters). URLs have four parts:

http:// www. enslow. com

| These letters tell the network what protocol, or language, to use. | These letters stand for World Wide Web. | This is the name of the company that owns the website. | These letters tell you what kind of website this is. Com stands for commercial. |

Getting to Websites

To get to a website, you use an application called a web browser. Some of the most popular browsers are Google Chrome, Firefox and Safari. Click on the icon for the browser to open a new window. Type the URL of the website into the address bar at the top.

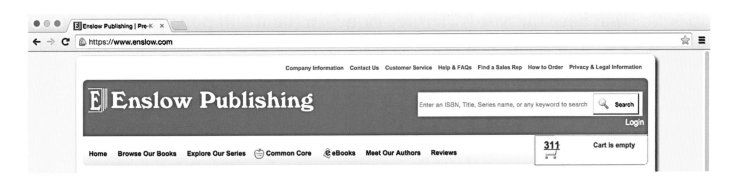

If you don't know the address to the website you want, your web browser will help you find it. Type in words that relate to the website you want to find. If you want to play a Disney game, type "Disney game" into the address bar. A list of websites that have the words "Disney game" in them will pop up. Click on the website you want.

Internet addresses that end in .gov are government websites. Those that end in .org usually belong to organizations.

To search for a website with Disney games like this one, just type "Disney game" into the address bar of a web browser.

Other Ways to Use the Internet

There are many uses for the Internet besides going to websites.

E-mail

Sending and receiving e-mails is one of the oldest ways to use the Internet. E-mail stands for electronic mail. The sender and receiver both need e-mail addresses. Each e-mail address has three parts.

jane @ enslow.com

This is the user name. This identifies the user of the e-mail address.

This symbol stands for the word "at." It separates the user name and the domain name.

This is the domain name. It tells the computer where to send the e-mail to reach the user.

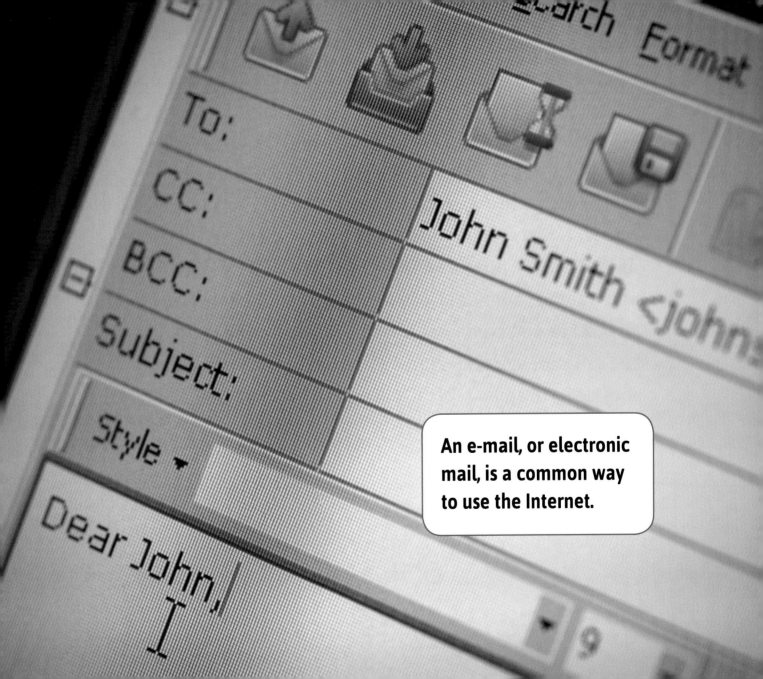

An e-mail, or electronic mail, is a common way to use the Internet.

Instant Messaging

Many people use instant messaging (IM) software to talk to each other over the Internet. Like texting on a cell phone, IM lets you see a message from someone right away. To talk with someone over IM, you and the person you want to communicate with must open the software first. Then you type a message into a small window that the software opens and press the enter or return key. Your message will appear on the other person's computer right away.

Making Phone Calls

More people are using the Internet to make phone calls. Internet phone calls work much differently than calls

using a cell phone or a home phone. They use VoIP. Pronounced VOYP, it stands for Voice over IP. VoIP calls are usually free. And you don't even need a telephone! You do need a computer with a microphone and a speaker, and so does the person you're calling.

VoIP systems are software programs that make phone calls to other computers. Two popular VoIP programs are

VoIP

Some VoIP programs, such as Skype, also let you make video calls so you can see your friends as you talk.

Google Voice and Skype. The software changes the sounds of a voice into binary numbers. The binary numbers are grouped into packets. The packets are sent through the Internet using TCP/IP. The receiving computer changes the binary numbers back into voice sounds. The sounds are played on a speaker.

Internet Safety

Because so many people use the Internet, you must be careful when you are online. Some people write programs called viruses that are meant to hurt computers or cause

People called hackers try to steal personal information from computers. Do not share your name, address, or phone number with anyone you talk to online.

trouble. Special software programs called virus scanners can protect your computer.

Nearly three billion people are connected to the Internet. It is the way people get information, watch movies, listen to music, and talk to each other. Go explore it for yourself!

To help you understand how the Internet works, it can be useful to see its parts. Go on a scavenger hunt at your house to find the equipment that lets your computer connect to the Internet! You will need the help of a parent, grandparent, or other adult.

Who Is Your ISP?

You know that Internet service is sold by an ISP, or Internet service provider. Who is your ISP? (Hint: It could be the same company that provides your phone or cable service.)

Find Your Modem

To connect to the Internet, a computer needs a modem. A modem is a tool that changes the computer language into sounds. Where is your modem, and what does it look like? (Hint: Modems are usually near a phone or cable connection.)

Try a Web Browser

To get online, you need to go through a web browser, such as Google Chrome, Internet Explorer, or Safari. Try opening a web browser on your computer. What happens? What do you do next? (Hint: See the next activity for ideas.)

Explore the Web

Choose one of the websites listed on page 24. Type the web address in the address bar of the web browser window and press the enter key. Once the web page appears, start clicking on different links to explore!

LEARN MORE

Books

Cosson, M.J., and Ronnie Rooney. *The Smart Kid's Guide to Using the Internet*. North Mankato, MN: The Child's World, 2014.

Lee, Sally. *Staying Safe Online*. Mankato, MN: Capstone Publishing, 2012.

Shea, John M. *Combating Computer Viruses*. New York: Gareth Stevens, 2013.

Websites

kidrex.org
A search engine just for kids!

kids.gov
Government website that features many topics, such as animals, history, art, and videos, that allow kids to safely explore some of what's available on the Internet.

netsmartzkids.org
Videos, games, and activity cards to teach kids how to be safe while online

INDEX

Published in 2016 by Enslow Publishing, LLC.
101 W. 23rd Street, Suite 240, New York, NY 10011

Copyright © 2016 by Enslow Publishing, LLC.
All rights reserved.

No part of this book may be reproduced by any means without the written permission of the publisher.

Library of Congress Cataloging-in-Publication Data
Yearling, Tricia, author.
    The internet : what it is and how to use it / Tricia Yearling.
        pages cm. — (Zoom in on technology)
    Audience: 5+
    Audience: Grades K to 3.
    Summary: "Describes the Internet, how it functions, and how to use it"— Provided by publisher.
    Includes bibliographical references and index.
    ISBN 978-0-7660-7382-1 (library binding)
    ISBN 978-0-7660-7380-7 (pbk.)
    ISBN 978-0-7660-7381-4 (6-pack)
    1. Internet—Juvenile literature. 2. World Wide Web—Juvenile literature. I. Title.
    TK5105.875.I57Y425 2016
    004.67'8—dc23
                                            2015033340

Printed in the United States of America

To Our Readers: We have done our best to make sure all website addresses in this book were active and appropriate when we went to press. However, the author and the publisher have no control over and assume no liability for the material available on those websites or on any websites they may link to. Any comments or suggestions can be sent by e-mail to customerservice@enslow.com.

Photo Credits: Cover, p. 1 Oleksiy mark/Shutterstock.com; Marish/Shutterstock.com (connectivity backgrounds and headers throughout book); p. 4 Blend Images/Shutterstock.com; p. 7 iStockphoto/RakicN; p. 8 iStockphoto.com/FuatKose; p. 10 iStockphoto.com/fieldwork; p. 11 dotshock/Shutterstock.com; pp. 12, 13, 16 Enslow Publishing; p. 15 GongTo/Shutterstock.com; p. 17 Pixel 4 Images/Shutterstock.com; p. 19 Lane Oatey/Blue Jean Images/Getty Images; p. 21 Rob Marmion/Shutterstock.com.